Howard had seen pictures of the pyramids in books. . . .

Seeing them in person was completely different! They rose like giants out of the desert sand. Their pointed tops shone brightly in the sunlight.

Howard wanted to spend more time sightseeing. But there was work to be done!

What kind of treasures were out there? Were noble mummies, decked with gold, lying in hidden tombs? If they were, could he figure out how to find them?

The most exciting, most inspiring,
most unbelievable stories . . .
are the ones that really happened!

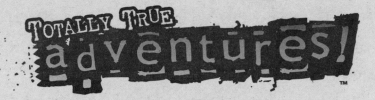

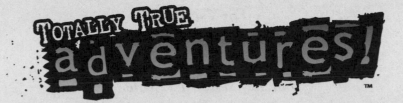

THE CURSE OF KING TUT'S MUMMY

By KATHLEEN WEIDNER ZOEHFELD

ILLUSTRATED BY JIM NELSON

A STEPPING STONE BOOK™
Random House 🏠 New York

For Geoff
—K.W.Z.

For my sister, Kristine
—J.N.

Special thanks to Dr. Deanna Kiser-Go.

Text copyright © 2007 by Kathleen Weidner Zoehfeld
Interior illustrations copyright © 2007 by Jim Nelson
Map art copyright © 2014 by Random House LLC
Photograph credits: pg. 101: (top) © martie1swart, some rights reserved; (bottom) © Rav560, some rights reserved. pg. 102: (top) © Darren Krape, some rights reserved; (bottom) © pareeerica, all rights reserved. pg. 103: (top) © ancientartpodcast.org, some rights reserved; (bottom) © qeaegypt, all rights reserved. pg. 104 © robinrimbaud, all rights reserved.

Visit us on the Web!
SteppingStonesBooks.com
randomhouse.com/kids

Educators and librarians, for a variety of teaching tools, visit us at
RHTeachersLibrarians.com

Library of Congress Cataloging-in-Publication Data
Zoehfeld, Kathleen Weidner.
The curse of King Tut's mummy / by Kathleen Weidner Zoehfeld ; illustrated by Jim Nelson.
p. cm.
"A Stepping Stone Book."
ISBN 978-0-375-83862-0 (pbk.) — ISBN 978-0-375-93862-7 (lib. bdg.)
1. Tutankhamen, King of Egypt—Tomb—Juvenile literature.
2. Carter, Howard, 1874–1939—Juvenile literature. 3. Egypt—Antiquities—Juvenile literature. I. Nelson, Jim, ill. II. Title.
DT87.5.Z64 2007   932'.014—dc22   2006017629

Printed in the United States of America   12 11

This book has been officially leveled by using the F&P Text Level Gradient™ Leveling System.

CONTENTS

1

A Dream of Royal Treasure

Howard Carter squeezed his father's hand. For as long as he could remember, he had wanted to visit Didlington Hall. Now he and his father stood before the great mansion. Seven tall stone statues of women with lion heads loomed over them. Howard felt as if their lion eyes were staring right at him.

Howard's father, Samuel, said that the

statues were over four thousand years old. They came from ancient Egypt. The Egyptian goddess of good health was always shown as a woman with a lion's head.

Good health was something Howard wished he had. He was a sickly boy. He was always too sick to go to school or play sports like other kids did. But he loved learning about art and history.

Howard ran his fingers over one of the goddess's feet. He counted her five toes. She wore bracelets on her ankles and a strange crown on her head.

Howard wanted to try drawing the statues. His father gave him pencils and paper. He sat down and began to sketch.

Samuel Carter, Howard's father, was a well-known artist. He had been hired to paint a portrait of the Amherst family.

They were the owners of Didlington Hall. Everyone said Howard shared his father's talent for art.

Didlington Hall was a wonderful place for a boy to spend time. The Amherst family had many old works of art. Their favorites were from ancient Egypt. While his father painted, Howard explored the huge house. Statues of gods and goddesses and beautiful tomb paintings filled every room.

One of the best treasures Howard saw wasn't made of gold or silver. It was four thin pieces from a papyrus scroll. Papyrus is a very old kind of paper first made in Egypt.

Howard couldn't read the writing on the papyrus. But Lord Amherst told him it was about royal tombs being robbed.

The most exciting part was a confession made by one of the robbers. He described what he and his friends saw in one of the tombs.

Lord Amherst read the man's words for Howard: "We . . . found the noble mummy of this king with his golden sword. A large number of golden charms and jewels were upon his neck. His crown of gold was upon him. The noble mummy of this king was completely bedecked with gold. His coffins were adorned with gold and silver inside and out."

The stories of tombs and treasure thrilled Howard. He wanted to learn all he could about Egypt's history. But Howard was the youngest of eleven children. The family didn't have enough money to send them all to college.

At the age of fifteen, Howard had to start working. In his journal, he wrote that he began painting "portraits of pet parrots, cats, and snappy, smelly lap-dogs." Howard had always loved animals. But painting rich people's pets was not exactly his dream come true!

His luck changed a couple of years later. Like his father, Howard became one of the Amherst family's favorite painters. When he was seventeen, friends of the Amhersts were looking for an artist to go with them to Egypt. The artist would help them copy the artwork on the walls of ancient tombs. The Amhersts told them about Howard Carter.

In 1891, Howard said goodbye to his father and mother. He could hardly believe he was really going to Egypt! A big ship with a steam engine and tall masts would take him there. But after a few hours on board, Howard was too sea-sick to care.

Finally, the ship reached the shores of Egypt. He was happy just to have his feet on dry land again. But he still had farther to go. The train ride to the city of Cairo was long and hot and lonely.

At the station, Howard met the people he would be working with—the Egypt Exploration Fund team. They took him to the three great pyramids at Giza. Howard had seen pictures of the pyramids in books. Seeing them in person was completely different! They rose like giants out of the desert sand. Their sloping sides and pointed tops shone brightly in the sunlight.

Howard wanted to spend more time sightseeing. But there was work to be done! The team members strapped their luggage on the backs of donkeys and set out on their trip. They rode through green farm fields to the bank of the Nile River. They crossed the Nile on a ferry. Several days later, as the sun was setting, they scrambled up a steep desert trail. At the trail's end, they reached a set of tombs carved out of the high cliffs. One of the bare-rock tombs would be Howard's new home.

He lay down on his bed. Unlike his soft mattress at home, this one was made of woven palm sticks. That night by candle-light, he scribbled in his journal. Was it a mistake to come to this gloomy place? Would the other team members like him? Would his paintings be good enough?

Howard soon settled into camp life and his new job. As he painted, his fears slowly went away.

For seven years, he copied tomb art. He studied Egyptian history and learned to read ancient Egyptian writing. And he had the chance to work with Sir William Matthew Flinders Petrie.

Petrie was an archaeologist—a scientist who studies the people and cultures of ancient times. He was famous for his careful, scientific work. Most others worked quickly once they found a site. They took only what looked valuable. Petrie went slowly.

As he worked, he made notes. He wrote down every detail about where and how and in what shape every single thing was found. Petrie didn't just gather treasures.

He wanted to find out all he could about ancient people's lives. Howard vowed to work like a scientist, too, not like a treasure hunter.

Still, on quiet evenings in camp, he looked out over the vast Egyptian desert. What kind of treasures were out there? Were noble mummies, "completely be-decked with gold," lying in hidden tombs? If they were, could he figure out how to find them?

2

THE MUMMY'S CURSE

Four thousand years ago, the mummies of an Egyptian official and his wife were buried. On the doorway of their tomb, the tomb-makers carved a warning. It said:

ALL PEOPLE WHO ENTER THIS TOMB,
WHO WILL MAKE EVIL AGAINST THIS TOMB,
AND DESTROY IT:
MAY THE CROCODILE BE

AGAINST THEM ON WATER,
AND SNAKES AGAINST THEM ON LAND.
MAY THE HIPPOPOTAMUS BE
AGAINST THEM ON WATER,
THE SCORPION AGAINST THEM ON LAND.

Like the official and his wife, most Egyptians believed that curses would stop tomb robbers. Sadly, the curses didn't work. Everywhere, tombs were broken into. The dishes and furniture, food and clothing inside were stolen. This was a disaster for an ancient Egyptian. Those everyday objects were supposed to be there for them after they died. They needed those comforts in the next world.

Unlike ordinary Egyptians, royal Egyptians had heaps of treasure to take with them. Pharaohs—Egyptian kings—knew they could not count on curses to protect their tombs. Around 2700 BC, the pharaohs began to build pyramids to hold their mummies and treasure. Priests and guards watched over them at all times.

But even with thick walls and royal guards, each and every pyramid was robbed. Later pharaohs built mazes and fake burial chambers in their pyramids. The mazes were supposed to confuse and frighten thieves. Sooner or later, these puzzling pyramids were robbed, too.

Finally, around 1550 BC, one king decided to try a different kind of tomb. Tuthmosis thought that pyramids acted like big markers. They told thieves exactly where to look. Instead of a fancy pyramid, he built a temple near the capital city of Thebes. There, people could come to honor him after he had died. But his tomb was hidden away in a secret place. He was sure no one would ever find it.

Farther to the west, across the Nile, was a dry, sandy valley. The valley's canyons were lined with high rocky cliffs. Tuthmosis ordered workmen to cut a tomb deep in the cliff walls.

After the king passed away, his servants gathered the things he would need in his afterlife. They packed his crowns, linen robes, jewels, golden thrones, beds, and scented oils. They wrapped up his favorite foods and fancy dishes to serve them on. They buried it all in his secret tomb.

Priests placed the king's mummy in his golden coffin. Then they laid the coffin in the tomb's burial chamber.

For the next five hundred years, other pharaohs wanted tombs like Tuthmosis's. They ordered that their mummies should be hidden in the same valley. People began to call it the Valley of the Tombs of the Kings. But in the end, robbers figured out where to look.

When he was a tomb painter, Howard Carter spent his free time taking long walks. He especially liked hiking through the Valley of the Kings. Before long, he got to know every nook and cranny.

He knew the stories of mummies putting curses on people. But to him it seemed that people were more of a curse on mummies. In fact, thieves *still* roamed the valley.

Carter could see that scientists like himself were in a serious race. If there was anything left in the valley, they had to find it—before the modern-day robbers did!

After eight years of hiking desert trails and camping under the stars, Howard Carter was no longer sickly. He was twenty-five years old when he got an important new job. He would be the Chief Inspector of Antiquities in Upper Egypt.

Just like today, many of the tombs in the valley were open to visitors. As chief inspector, one of his duties was to keep those tombs safe and in good repair. Also, he had to watch over the people who were allowed to dig in the valley.

Most of the experts believed that all the tombs in the valley had already been found. They hoped to uncover more artifacts. But they felt that the really great treasures had been dug out or stolen long ago. Over the next few years, Carter began to think they were wrong. He believed that the tomb of at least one more pharaoh still lay hidden somewhere in the valley!

3

ENTER
LORD CARNARVON

Carter's new job kept him so busy, he hardly had any time to explore. He wondered if he would ever have a chance to search for that tomb. If everything had gone well, maybe he never would have. But one afternoon, a bunch of rude tourists got into a fight with the guards at one of the tombs. That day Carter's life changed forever.

He asked the rowdy visitors to leave. They demanded to be let into the tomb. The guards tried to block their way. The tourists threw chairs. They swung their walking sticks at the guards.

Carter ordered the guards to defend the tomb. In the struggle, two of the tourists were hurt. They stormed away and threatened to take the matter to court. Carter was angry. The tourists had attacked Egyptian guards! They had damaged walls and broken chairs! He believed *they* should be taken to court.

Carter's boss didn't agree. He told Carter that he should say he was sorry for giving the order that started the fight. Carter refused. He was stubborn. When he believed he was right about something, he never budged.

Although his boss liked him, he asked Carter to quit the job. Upset, Carter went back to a quiet life of painting. After three years, he was broke. He had barely enough money to pay his rent. His old boss worried about him. Then he had a brilliant idea. He introduced Carter to George Edward Stanhope Molyneux Herbert, the fifth Earl of Carnarvon.

Lord Carnarvon was born into one of the richest families in England. He and his wife lived in a magnificent castle called Highclere. The castle was surrounded by 36,000 acres of shaded lawns, gardens, thickets, and wild woods.

During the first part of his life, Lord Carnarvon spent most of his time racing horses and fast cars. But in 1901, at the age of thirty-five, he was badly hurt in a car accident. He never really got better. From that time on, he walked with a cane. Because his chest had been crushed in the accident, he had trouble breathing. And he was always catching a cold or the flu.

Lord Carnarvon's doctor told him the damp English winters weren't good for his health. The warm, dry weather of Egypt would be better. So Lord and Lady Carnarvon went to Egypt. After one winter, Lord Carnarvon was bored. He grumped that he had nothing to do. One of his friends said he should study ancient Egypt. After reading a few books, Lord Carnarvon was hooked.

The next winter he hired a crew. Soon they were hard at work, searching the desert for treasures. After six weeks of labor under the hot desert sun, they had found only one thing—the mummy of a cat in its wooden coffin!

Even though he didn't find much, Lord Carnarvon loved the work. He was sure that all he needed was the advice of a "learned expert." With a little help, he knew he would find gold.

Howard Carter was exactly the expert that Lord Carnarvon needed. And Lord Carnarvon was exactly the right person to pay for the search Carter wanted to try. Carter's old boss enjoyed seeing these two men meet for the first time, in 1908. He sensed that the easygoing lord and the hot-tempered archaeologist would make an interesting team.

4

THE MYSTERIOUS
PHARAOH

Howard Carter and Lord Carnarvon couldn't wait to start digging in the Valley of the Kings. Unfortunately, an American millionaire, Theodore Davis, already had the permit. The Egyptian government let only one team dig in the valley at a time. Like it or not, Carter and Carnarvon had to wait.

In 1914, Davis finally decided to quit.

He swore that the valley was empty. There were no more tombs to be found. Howard Carter and Lord Carnarvon did not believe *that*. They leapt at the chance!

By early the next year, they were allowed to dig in the valley. First they had to finish up some work Davis had left behind. Carter was already daydreaming about one pharaoh in particular. His name was Tutankhamun, or King Tut.

Carter had studied Egyptian history since he was a kid. He knew the time period when King Tut ruled. Tut came to the throne after King Akhenaten. Carter remembered the sculptures he had seen of Akhenaten. They were unforgettable!

In them, Akhenaten had narrow eyes, a long head, and a pear-shaped body. Ancient artists showed him with his beautiful wife,

Nefertiti, and their six pear-shaped, long-headed daughters. Their rule was a very strange time in Egypt's history.

Akhenaten felt that Egyptian priests were getting too powerful. So he banned all the gods the Egyptian people were used to worshiping. He created a new religion with only one god. And he closed the priests' temples. Akhenaten and his family moved out of the capital city of Thebes. They built a new capital city to the north. The Egyptian people were angry, but they followed their ruler's wishes.

As soon as Akhenaten died, the royal family moved back to Thebes. Tutankhamun became the new king. He was only nine years old!

Usually a king's oldest son becomes king when his father dies. Was King Tut Akhenaten's son? Carter was not sure. He did know that, at the age of eight, Tut married one of Akhenaten's daughters. It wasn't unusual for a king's son to marry his sister or half sister!

As soon as Tut became king, the temples in Thebes opened again. Life in Egypt went back to normal. The old priests were happy. Was the young king glad to move back to Thebes? Or was he forced to return by more powerful men? King Tut's life was a mystery.

No one had ever found Akhenaten's mummy. But historians knew that King Akhenaten ordered his tomb to be built near his own capital city. When Tut died, did he want to be buried in the Valley of the Kings? Or did he ask to be buried near his father's city, many miles to the north? King Tut's burial was a mystery, too.

Theodore Davis had found one clue in the valley that Carter thought was interesting. It was a special chamber that seemed to have been made for Akhenaten's mummy. A coffin lay in the chamber. The coffin had Akhenaten's name carved on it. Someone must have tried to move his mummy to the valley.

Davis found pieces of pottery on the floor of the chamber. Carter looked at them closely. They were marked with King Tut's name. From this, Carter decided that Tut was the one who tried to move Akhenaten. Maybe, if King Tut wanted his father's mummy moved to the valley, he wanted his own tomb to be there, too. But lots of tombs lay in the valley. What made Carter think Tut's hadn't been robbed like all the others?

He was thinking of the dusty old papyrus at Didlington Hall. Ancient Egyptians kept careful records of tomb robberies in the valley. None of them mentioned Tut's tomb. Carter felt a glimmer of hope. Maybe—just maybe—it had never been looted at all!

5

HOWARD CARTER, DETECTIVE

Carter often told people that if he had not become an archaeologist, he would have been a detective. But trying to find a hidden tomb in a vast desert valley would be hard even for the best detective in the world. Where should he begin? If he was going to find King Tut's tomb, he'd need more clues.

He looked at Davis's notes and studied

the other items he had found. Were there any clues that might tell him exactly where King Tut was?

Davis wrote that one day in 1906, a large tilted rock caught the eye of his assistant. Something about it seemed out of place. Davis asked his workers to lift it. Under it was a beautiful light blue cup. As he wiped it clean, he was startled to see Tut's name on it.

He ordered his team to search the area. Soon they discovered what looked like the entrance to a tomb. They dug down through an ancient tunnel. Deep underground, they came to a mysterious room. It was filled with dried mud from an old flood. Davis thought treasures might be hidden in the mud.

They sifted through the dirt. All they found was a small statue of a man and a broken wooden box. The box held a few pieces of gold foil with Tut's name on them.

Davis told everyone he had found King Tut's tomb. But it was a big disappointment. All the king's treasures had been cleared out ages ago.

A few days after they found the mud-filled room, Davis's team uncovered fifteen large pottery jars. They had been buried in a deep pit. The pit was just a few steps away from the underground room. Davis noted that Tut's name was on some of the jars. They didn't hold any gold or jewels. What was inside just looked like trash. He put the jars in storage.

Carter never had a chance to study the jars. But he thought a lot about that small, mud-filled room. He decided Davis's idea that it was a tomb was ridiculous! No Egyptian pharaoh would have such a plain, simple tomb. But Carter thought the room might be a clue. Maybe the king had used it for storage. Tut's real tomb must be somewhere nearby.

Those pieces of gold and the blue cup bothered him, though. None of the old papers mentioned a robbery of King Tut's

tomb. But there might have been a robbery that officials forgot to write about. Maybe there *had* been thieves. Maybe they had left these pieces behind as they made their escape.

Carter was worried as he and Lord Carnarvon worked. Soon it would be summer. The Egyptian desert would become sizzling hot—too hot for any more digging. Every summer, archaeologists gave their crews time off. Carter and Lord Carnarvon decided to spend the summer at Highclere Castle. But even when he was on vacation, Carter didn't stop thinking about King Tut.

He drew a map of the Valley of the Kings. Many treasure hunters had combed the valley over the years. But Carter felt they had searched in a random way. He would search like a scientist—like his old hero, Flinders Petrie.

He drew a triangle on his map. Based on the clues in Davis's work, he believed King Tut's tomb was somewhere in that triangle.

6

SEASONS OF
DUST AND SAND

In the fall of 1917, Howard Carter and Lord Carnarvon went back to Egypt. Carter measured out his triangle on the desert floor. Bit by bit, they would clean away the rubble. Then they would dig down to the bedrock. Carter was eager to begin. As long as he was digging, he didn't have time to worry.

Lord Carnarvon couldn't believe the

work that was ahead of them! He thought about the steam shovels and bulldozers back in England. They could move tons of rubble a day. But even Lord Carnarvon couldn't afford to bring big machines like those to the desert.

Their crew of young boys and men would have to move all the soil, gravel, and rocks using only picks and shovels. Lord Carnarvon would pay them by the number of baskets they filled and carried away each day.

They began clearing a section of Carter's magic triangle, close to the tomb of King Ramses VI. As they were digging, they found some stone walls. Carter knew they were very old. They seemed to be the foundations for a group of small huts. Long ago, these little buildings had probably been the homes for workers while they built Ramses's tomb. Carter decided to leave them alone. He asked his workers to move to another part of the triangle.

For months, they dug and dug. But for all their work, they found only dust and sand and rocks.

Carter and Lord Carnarvon returned with high hopes the next fall. Lady Carnarvon came along, too. In that whole second season, all they found were thirteen stone jars. Lady Carnarvon thought the jars were beautiful. She dug them out of the ground herself. Still, they didn't give any clues about King Tut's tomb.

The next fall, they got ready for a third season. After months of backbreaking labor, they found—nothing. A season like that made finding thirteen jars look good. They slumped home to England for the summer, empty-handed.

Carter wondered how they were going to get up the energy for another season. But they did. In the fourth season, they moved more rock and rubble. They didn't find a thing.

Carter wasn't worrying anymore. He was getting depressed. Everyone told him the valley was empty. Why hadn't he listened? He knew Lord Carnarvon was tired of paying a big crew to move rocks.

Should they give the valley another try? They began their fifth season without even daring to hope. Then Carter heard from an old friend. Herbert Winlock worked at the Metropolitan Museum of Art in New York. He told Carter that he had finally had a chance to study Davis's fifteen pottery jars. They were not boring at all!

The seals on the jars had Tut's name on them. What Winlock found inside was amazing! He went through all the items in the jars. And he realized that he was looking at the remains of a great feast.

He figured that eight people had gone

to the funeral of the king. They wore floral neck wreaths and linen headbands. Between them they had eaten five ducks, two plovers, and a leg of lamb. Their cups had been filled with beer and wine.

When they were done eating, they cleaned up. With two small brooms, they swept up their crumbs. They stuffed everything into the jars. Then they dug a pit and buried them, leaving the desert neat and tidy behind them.

Winlock's news came as a ray of hope. Certainly King Tut must lie nearby! But spring came. The weather got hotter, and Carter and Lord Carnarvon still had found nothing. The gloomy mood returned. It hung over them like a dark cloud.

7

One Last Chance

In the summer of 1922, Howard Carter headed to Highclere Castle, once again. He looked forward to relaxing with Lord and Lady Carnarvon and their daughter, Evelyn. This summer, though, Lord Carnarvon dreaded his friend's visit. He steeled himself to tell Carter some bad news.

Lord Carnarvon invited Carter into his private library. They sat beside the marble fireplace, as usual. But Lord Carnarvon didn't ask excitedly about their plans for next season. Instead, he told his friend that he couldn't spend any more money digging in the Valley of the Kings.

Carter wasn't surprised. It had been five years. Nothing had gone well for them in the valley. Still, he pulled out their old map. He pointed out the one area they hadn't tried yet—the spot near the ancient huts.

Lord Carnarvon just shook his head. It was time to quit. Carter said he understood. He couldn't blame him. But Carter wasn't ready to give up. Not until he had dug up every single square inch of his triangle! Carter told Carnarvon he had saved a little money over the years. He had enough to pay the crew himself.

Lord Carnarvon was touched by his friend's determination. As far as he could tell, they were out of luck. But he knew Carter meant exactly what he said. Lord Carnarvon didn't have the heart to let his partner go it alone. He agreed to give it one last try.

So Carter sailed back to Egypt in October. Before he got on the train to the valley, he bought a pet canary. He imagined a long, lonely season ahead of him. The yellow bird would cheer him up.

Carter's Egyptian housekeeper and his three foremen were happy to see him coming home. They smiled when they saw the pretty little pet. "The bird of gold will bring us good luck!" they cried. "This year we will find a tomb of gold!"

By November 1, Carter and his foremen had hired their crew. Carter made drawings of all the huts and took photos of them. Then he ordered the crew to remove them. By the end of the third day, they had dug down to the layer of rubble under the huts.

On the morning of November 4, total silence greeted Carter as he walked to the dig site. He was worried. Had someone been hurt? Suddenly he saw the water boy running toward him. The boy could barely hold back his excitement.

Every day the boy filled his big pottery jars with water for the crew. Then he carried the jars to the site and buried them in sand to keep them cool. He told Mr. Carter how he had filled all his jars with water early that morning. Then he got down on his knees, just as he always did.

He dug the hole for the first jar. But instead of soft sand, his hands brushed against solid rock. He scooped the sand away from the rock. And . . . Well, Mr. Carter would have to come see for himself!

The boy grabbed Carter's coat sleeve and pulled him to the spot where he'd been digging. Could it be the first step in a stairway leading down to a tomb? What did Mr. Carter think?

Could it be? It seemed too good to be true! Carter knelt down and brushed more sand away. "Yes," he gasped. He stared at the smooth stone under his hand. "This is the tomb."

He gave the order, and everyone began to dig. A day and a half passed quickly. Their baskets full of rubble seemed lighter than ever before. Soon they were laughing in excitement at what was in front of their eyes. They could see the outline of a staircase!

The workers uncovered step after step. Twelve steps down, they came to a mysterious door. The door was made of stone blocks. The blocks had been covered with a smooth coat of plaster.

Pressed into the plaster was an oval-shaped mark. It had a picture of a jackal on it. Under the jackal were nine humans bound with ropes. In an instant, Carter knew—it was the seal of the Necropolis! That was the mark of the priests who guarded the royal burial grounds. Carter looked closely and saw more royal seals.

Their meaning was clear. Someone of great importance had been buried here! The years of hard work were going to be rewarded after all! Carter searched for a seal with the name of the person buried in the tomb. But he couldn't find one.

He opened a small peephole in the door. Through it he saw what looked like a passage leading down. It was filled with rubble. That didn't worry Carter. The rubble would make it hard for them to get in. But it proved that someone had gone to the trouble of trying to keep robbers out.

What treasures would they find beyond that rubble-filled passage? Carter said it took every bit of self-control to keep from breaking down the door! He tore himself away. Then he ordered his crew to fill the stairway back in with sand.

Twenty-two years he had waited for this discovery. Now he had to wait just a little longer. He wanted Lord Carnarvon to come from England. They would open the door together.

Early the next morning, he sent Lord Carnarvon a telegram: "At last have made wonderful discovery in Valley. A magnificent tomb with seals intact. Re-covered same for your arrival. Congratulations!"

8

THE TOMB OF THE GOLDEN BIRD

The next day, Carter stared at the spot. The stairway was hidden again, under the sand. Had it all been just a dream?

Lord Carnarvon had sent an answer. He and his daughter, Evelyn, would hurry to Egypt as fast as they could. Even so, it would take them two weeks.

To Carter, it felt like forever! To calm his nerves, he made a list. If the tomb ended up being as important as he hoped, he was going to need help. He wrote down the names of all the experts he knew. He sent a telegram to one of his best friends, Arthur Callender. Callender was busy at another site in Egypt. But Carter asked him to drop his work and come right away.

As soon as Callender showed up, Carter left for Cairo to meet the Carnarvons. Carter invited Callender to stay at his house. He asked him to look after his canary while he was gone. But one afternoon, Callender heard an awful fluttering sound. He rushed into the room where the canary was kept. A cobra had slipped into its cage. The deadly snake was gulping the poor bird down, headfirst!

In ancient Egypt, the cobra was a

symbol of the pharaoh's power. Callender was sad that Carter's little pet had died. But Carter's housekeeper and foremen were horrified. They thought it was a sign of terrible things to come.

If there was some pharaoh's dark curse hanging over them, everyone soon forgot all about it. They were bubbling with excitement as they led Lord Carnarvon and Lady Evelyn to the site. In honor of the canary, the workmen nicknamed it "The Tomb of the Golden Bird."

After two days of work, they had cleared the stairs completely. There were sixteen steps in all. Now the whole door was uncovered. Carter knelt down to study the marks on the lower part. He saw a few more of the Necropolis seals. But here he spotted different marks, too.

They were the royal seals of King Tut!

Carter's mood bounced back and forth between joy and doubt. He noticed that the upper left-hand corner of the door had been opened in ancient times. In fact, it looked as if it had been broken and patched up twice. Had thieves gotten in?

The door had been resealed both times by the priests of the Necropolis. Carter thought this was a good sign. If all the king's treasures had been stolen, the priests wouldn't have bothered to seal the tomb up again.

Carter and his team sifted through every handful of sand from the stairway. They found pieces of broken pottery, bits of wooden boxes—all sorts of odds and ends. A few had Tut's name on them. But many were marked with other kings' names. Carter worried. Maybe they had not found a tomb at all. Maybe this was just a storage room.

After they took down the door, Carter faced the rubble-filled passage. There, too, he saw signs of looting. The stone chips in the passage were white. But the gravel that filled the upper left-hand corner was a little darker. Someone had dug a tunnel through the white stone chips. Then the guards had filled in the tunnel with a different kind of gravel.

Carter and his team sorted all the rubble, one basketful at a time. Every piece of pottery, wood, or leather was important. Even the smallest bead could be a clue.

Carter traced two trails of clues. One was on the floor of the passage. The other was along the narrow tunnel.

These little bits of wood and pottery must have been left by two sets of thieves. Carter imagined the first set dropping and breaking some of their loot as they ran out the open passage. Then, after the guards had filled the passage with gravel, the second set of thieves snuck in. Carter imagined them dropping and breaking things as they wriggled out, like rats, through their tunnel.

At the end of the long passage, Carter found another door. It looked a lot like the first one. Just as Carter feared, that door had been broken into also. Like the outer door, the inner door had been fixed. The priests had resealed it.

Finally, the team had cleared away the last bits of gravel. Carter took pictures of the inner door. Then the unbelievable moment arrived. Callender handed Carter a long iron rod. With trembling hands, Carter pried the first stone loose. Would they find anything inside?

Carter poked the rod through the small opening he had made. He waved it around. As far as he could tell, there was only empty space and darkness. He lit a candle and held it up to the opening. The candle flame flickered in the hot air flowing out.

Carter made the hole a little wider and stuck the candle through it. He peered in. Lord Carnarvon and Lady Evelyn stood anxiously by his side. Carter was silent. His eyes got used to the dim light. Then beautiful forms began to take shape. "Strange animals, statues, and gold—everywhere the glint of gold."

Lord Carnarvon couldn't wait any longer. "Can you see anything?" he cried.

It was all Carter could do to get out the words. "Yes, wonderful things!"

9

THE OPENING OF THE TOMB

The next day, they began to take down the inner door. When the opening was wide enough, Howard Carter, Lady Evelyn, Lord Carnarvon, and Arthur Callender stepped into the tomb. Inside they smelled sweet perfume and ancient oils. They were breathing the same air that had been in that room for over three thousand years!

A garland of dried flowers lay on the floor. An oil lamp sat on the floor near the door. The friends and family who went to the king's funeral had used the lamp to light their way through the dark tomb. It was as if they had left only yesterday!

In awe, Carter and Lord Carnarvon moved their flashlight beams from one treasure to the next. Golden thrones. Boxes decorated with lovely scenes of Egyptian life. Fancy white vases. Three magnificent couches, their golden sides made in the shapes of long animals with weird heads. A pile of golden chariots. Never before had anyone found so much treasure in one place!

To calm himself and sort out his thoughts, Carter took notes. He carefully removed the rest of the stones in the doorway. Callender put in electric lights. Suddenly the whole room was flooded with light. Other treasures, one more beautiful than the next, seemed to leap out of the shadows.

They studied everything closely. Down on his hands and knees, Lord Carnarvon found a hole. Someone had broken through the wall under one of the animal couches. He and Carter crawled through into another room. It was a mess!

Someone had tossed delicate jars, golden boxes, games, baskets of fruit, chairs, and golden beds this way and that. Not one inch of floor space was free of clutter. Carter believed the thieves had made the hole. They had pawed through everything in this room, searching for gold and jewels.

In the first room, everything was neater. The robbers had been here, too, of course. But someone, probably the priests, had tidied up. Lady Evelyn took a close look at two life-sized statues of the king. They stood facing each other on opposite sides of one wall. The two statues seemed to be guarding a square section of the wall. Lady Evelyn could see that it had been plastered over. And it was marked with the seal of the Necropolis!

Carter came to see. Right away he knew. This was another door! Maybe it would lead to another passage and more rooms. Maybe the passage would lead to a room holding the mummy of King Tut!

Or would it? Part of the door at the bottom looked like it had been broken open and fixed long ago—just like the first two doors. Had the king's mummy been moved?

Every single thing in the first room would have to be taken out by Carter and his team. Only then could they even think about opening other rooms. But

Carter, Lord Carnarvon, Callender, and Lady Evelyn were curious. They decided to make a small hole in the door where the thieves had broken in.

Carter squeezed through first. He had a big surprise. There was no passage leading to other rooms. Instead, he was face to face with a magnificent shrine. It was made of carved wood. The heavy wooden sides were covered with gold. Brilliant blue glittered through, where the wood had been carved into beautiful designs.

The big double doors of the shrine were not locked. Two ebony bolts held the doors shut. Slowly, Carter drew back the bolts. The doors swung open. There, inside, was another golden shrine. The doors of this shrine were bound shut with rope. The knot held the seal of the Necropolis.

Carter's heart leapt! That knot must have been made on the day of the king's funeral. No one had handled it since.

Once again, Carter remembered the papyrus at Didlington Hall. It told of golden shrines like these. There could be up to five shrines here—each one nested inside the other. And at the center? It must be King Tut, completely bedecked in gold. Untouched by thieves! Exactly as he had been laid to rest, more than three thousand years ago!

Just off the shrine room was another room. This room held some of the most important treasures of all. The first thing they saw was a large dark statue of the jackal god—the guardian of the dead. Behind the jackal was another shrine so beautiful it made them gasp. Carter knew

what it was. This special golden chest held the mummified liver, lungs, stomach, and intestines of the king.

There were many smaller shrines, too. And statues. Boxes of jewelry. Beautiful model boats. Parts of chariots. The room was filled to the brim. It was too wonderful to be true!

They could hardly bear it when they had to leave. They wriggled out of the hole they'd made. They put the stones back in place. Then they plastered over the hole. It would be weeks before they opened the door for everyone to see. They vowed to keep their sneak peek a secret.

Carter and Callender locked up the tomb. They went back to Carter's house. Carter wrote to the experts on his list. He would need them all now!

Meanwhile, Lord Carnarvon ordered supplies. They'd have to photograph every piece of treasure in place—exactly as they found it. Each item would have to be preserved with wax or chemicals. Then everything would have to be carefully packed. All the treasure would be shipped to the museum in Cairo. The job ahead of them was huge!

10

KING TUT'S TOMB— CURSE OR BLESSING?

By the middle of December, Carter's team of experts met him in the valley. Over the next few weeks, they helped him carry all the treasures in the first room to a special laboratory. The lab was set up in an empty tomb in a quiet corner of the valley. There they took pictures of each item again. They fixed parts that were broken or fragile. And they stored everything safely until it was time to go to the museum.

By the middle of February, the only things left in the first room were the two statues of the king. They stood there like soldiers, watching over that "mysterious" third door. Carter, Lady Evelyn, Callender, and Lord Carnarvon had not breathed a word to anyone about how they had broken in. No one knew about the golden shrines.

On February 16, Carter led a small group of officials down the sixteen steps. Lord Carnarvon had ordered folding chairs set up in the empty room. As soon as everyone was settled, the drama began.

Carter and Lord Carnarvon removed the stones from the doorway one by one. For thousands of years, King Tut's golden shrines sat in darkness and silence. Now Carter would open the door and show them to the world.

The people nearly fell off their chairs in wonder. They had seen golden shrines in ancient paintings. But no one had ever imagined they would see one in real life!

Once the word was out, everyone wanted a tour of the tomb. Newspaper reporters, government officials, museum directors, princes and queens from other lands. Everyone begged Carter and Lord Carnarvon to let them have a look. By the end of February, Carter and Lord Carnarvon were worn out. They closed the tomb for the season.

Lady Evelyn took her father to a quiet hotel in Cairo for a rest. But he seemed to grow more tired as the days went by. In the middle of March, Lady Evelyn sent Carter a letter with bad news. Her father had been bitten on the cheek by a mosquito. He'd cut the bite with his razor when he was shaving. Now the bite was badly infected. She told Carter that her father was in bed with a fever.

A few days later, the fever was worse. Lady Carnarvon hurried to Cairo with their family doctor. Carter rushed to Cairo, too. But it was too late. Today we have medicines to cure infections—but not in those days. Weakened by the infection, Lord Carnarvon caught pneumonia. On April 5, early in the morning, he died.

Newspapers said the lights went out in Cairo that morning. It was pretty common for the lights to go out in Cairo then. Still, many believed *this* blackout was a bad omen.

Lord Carnarvon's son told people that his father's faithful dog, Susie, died that same morning. Some people wondered—had the death of the golden bird really been a sign of evil things to come?

When Lord Carnarvon died, newspapers ran stories about it. That day, headlines shouted: "The Curse of the Pharaoh Takes Its First Victim!"

A novelist said she had an ancient book in her library. It told of "dire punishments" for anyone who dared disturb a tomb. She didn't say what those punishments were. But it all sounded very dark and creepy.

Many different stories were printed. One said that King Tut's golden shrine had a curse written on it. "For those who enter the sacred tomb, the wings of death will visit them quickly."

Another newspaper story said that a

small mud brick found near the jackal god held a curse. "I will kill all those who cross this threshold."

The stories of curses were all made up. The words on the shrine are a common prayer. And the mud brick says, "I am the one who stops sand from blocking the secret chamber."

People were thrilled by the scary stories. But none of them were true.

Howard Carter thought the stories were silly. He had lost his partner and his best friend. And there was so much work ahead! He wondered how he would do it all without Lord Carnarvon's help. But he didn't believe in the mummy's curse.

In his heart, Carter knew that his old friend had felt blessed, not cursed. He had lived to see his dream come true.

II

UNWRAPPING KING TUT'S MUMMY

Carter felt sorry that Lord Carnarvon wouldn't be there when they opened King Tut's shrines. All that summer, he wondered about the king. What would he look like? Would there be gold and jewels sealed up in the coffin with him?

Carter returned to Egypt in October 1925 to begin the hardest work of his life. That fall, the desert just wouldn't cool off.

On some days, the temperature hit 120 degrees in the shade. But every day, Carter and his team went down into the roasting-hot chamber.

They opened the doors of the first shrine. Then Carter cut the knotted rope on the doors of the second shrine. They swung open. Shining inside was a third golden shrine. Carter opened those doors. Just as the old papyrus had described, there was a fourth golden shrine inside that one!

No one was able to speak. They read the words of the king, written on the doors. "I have seen yesterday. I know tomorrow."

The past and the future were about to meet. Carter pulled the doors open. There before them was the most wonder-ful sight yet. A huge sarcophagus carved out of beautiful red stone! On each corner was a winged goddess. The four goddesses seemed to be protecting the dead king.

Carter knew the king's coffin would be inside. But there wasn't enough room to lift the lid of the sarcophagus. First, they had to take out the wooden shrines, one plank at a time. In the tight space, they bumped their heads and pinched their fingers. They squeezed in and out like weasels and worked in all kinds of crazy positions.

Once the shrines were out, Carter and his team rigged up ropes and pulleys. They hoisted the heavy stone lid of the sarcophagus.

Carter peered in. At first, he saw only darkness. Emptiness!

He soon realized that his eyes had been fooled by a dark linen cloth. It covered the coffin completely. His hands trembled as he reached in. He rolled back the cloth. The coffin was the loveliest thing he had ever seen. It was covered in glowing gold. The whole coffin was made in the image of the young pharaoh. His dark, quiet eyes gazed up at them. His hands were folded across his chest.

Inside this large coffin was another coffin. And inside that one, yet another!

Carter and his team decided to raise

the coffins out of the sarcophagus. They were shocked at how heavy the coffins were. Then Carter realized the inner coffin was made of solid gold. No one had ever seen anything like it before!

Finally, the moment came to open the last coffin. Carter was about to meet the king he had dreamed of as a child at Didlington Hall. The king he had searched for for so long. They lifted the solid-gold lid.

King Tut's mummy rested inside, just as he had for more than three thousand years. Carter and his team slowly unwrapped the king's linen bandages. They found many golden charms hidden in them. The king had a golden mask over his head. He wore a golden crown. And he had a golden dagger tucked into his golden belt. He wore sparkling jeweled bracelets and collars. A pair of golden sandals was on his feet.

When Carter looked into the face of the king, he saw a young boy. A boy about the same age he had been when he sailed to Egypt for the first time. Time, said Carter, seemed to vanish. He touched the king's face with his own hands.

For a moment, he imagined the king's young wife and all the people who had come to his funeral. It was as if he could hear their ghostly footsteps departing.

For the rest of Carter's life, the memories of that day stayed with him. He spent eight more years taking care of all the treasures and getting them safely to the Cairo Museum.

The scary headlines never stopped. Every now and then, something bad would happen to someone who had seen the tomb. Then newspapers ran stories about "The Curse of the Pharaoh!" Carter never paid attention to stories of curses. He lived a long life.

After his work in Egypt was done, he moved back to England. He began to write about his adventures in the Valley of the Kings. Wherever he went, people wanted to hear about King Tut.

Carter left the king's mummy resting quietly in his tomb. But Tut's fame spread around the world. Millions of people came to Egypt to visit his mummy and his treasures.

Magazines and newspapers brought pictures to those who couldn't visit. The artwork was unforgettable. An Egyptian craze began. Everyone wanted clothes, jewelry, sandals, and hairdos in ancient

Egyptian style! People couldn't stop talking about King Tut.

Today people still love King Tut and all his treasures. The once-forgotten boy king has become the most famous Egyptian pharaoh of all!

AUTHOR'S NOTE

The powerful men who ruled after King Tut chipped his name off his public monuments. They wanted to erase his name from history. That was probably because he was the son of the much-hated King Akhenaten.

Did these same men murder the young king? A CT scan of King Tut's mummy gave scientists clues about how he died. But there are still many questions.

The bone just above his left knee was broken. Maybe it was broken after he died. But most scientists think the king broke his leg while he was alive. It never had a chance to heal. No one dies of a broken leg. But the break was so serious, it could have gotten infected. Did King Tut die of an infection caused by a broken leg?

The front part of King Tut's ribs was cut away. This is very mysterious, too. Maybe the priests removed the ribs when they mummified the king. Or maybe the young king had a bad accident during a battle or a hunting trip. The same accident that broke his leg might have also crushed his chest.

The scan of the king's skull is interesting. Some people once thought that King Tut was murdered by a blow to the head. The scan proves that theory wrong. It shows no wounds in his skull. So no one snuck into his room at night and clobbered him on the head.

We may never know exactly how King Tut died. But the scan has given us more clues. And now artists have all the information they need to show us King Tut's face. Through them, we can see the boy king, almost exactly as he would have looked in life.

A Note About the Canary

Some people have doubted the story of Carter's canary. In 1922, a friend said the bird was eaten by a cobra. A year and a half later, another friend wrote in her journal that Carter gave her his canary. He wanted her to look after it while he was in England that summer. Was the bird really alive? Or did Carter buy another canary to lift the gloomy mood after the first bird died? It's a mystery that may never be fully solved!

THE STORY BEHIND THE STORY

THE CURSE OF KING TUT'S MUMMY

EGYPT

Egypt is a country in Africa, bordered on the north by the Mediterranean Sea and on the east by the Red Sea, and split by the Nile, the

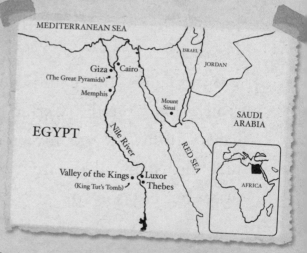

world's longest river. Egypt has been settled since ancient times, over 7,000 years! Ancient Egypt was the home of an advanced culture that built pyramids, developed a writing system, and was ruled by pharaohs like King Tut.

EGYPTIAN WRITING

Ancient Egyptian writing is called hieroglyphics. As time passed, people forgot how to read hieroglyphics. By the 1700s, no one could read them anymore. Then, in 1799, troops in Napoléon's army found the Rosetta Stone. Carved into the Rosetta Stone were the same words in three languages, including Greek and hieroglyphics. Since people could read Greek, they figured out the hieroglyphics, too. But it wasn't easy. We have twenty-six letters in the English language—Egyptians had over 2,000 hieroglyphics!

PYRAMIDS

Before pharaohs were buried in the Valley of the Kings, their tombs were in the pyramids. The three Pyramids at Giza were built over 4,000 years ago. Around two million limestone blocks make up the largest pyramid—and each block weighs between two and fifteen tons! That pyramid is the tomb of the pharaoh Khufu. It has three burial chambers, and Khufu was buried in one of them. Sliding blocks were put in place to keep out thieves, but it didn't work. The tomb was looted long ago.

TOMB OF TREASURE

It's hard to say what the value of the treasure in King Tut's tomb is. Many of the objects are one of a kind. The solid gold coffin alone may be worth millions!

Some people are surprised when they see photographs of how jumbled up the treasure was. Historians think that the tomb had been robbed twice in ancient times and then resealed by priests. The priests didn't bother to tidy it up.

Howard Carter circa 1924

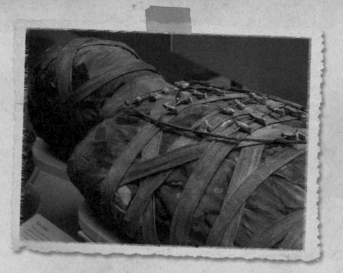

MUMMIES

How did Egyptians make a mummy? First, when a pharaoh died, the body was washed with river water and wine. Then the lungs, liver, stomach, and intestines were taken out and packed in jars. The brains were removed through his nose. The body was covered with a kind of salt to dry it. After forty days, it was washed with perfumes and stuffed with herbs, spices, and sawdust to give it a rounder shape. Then it was wrapped in linen strips, starting with the fingers and toes. A golden mask was placed over the face, and the mummy was settled into a coffin. This coffin was lowered within another coffin and another and then put into a stone sarcophagus. It took around seventy days to prepare a pharaoh for burial!

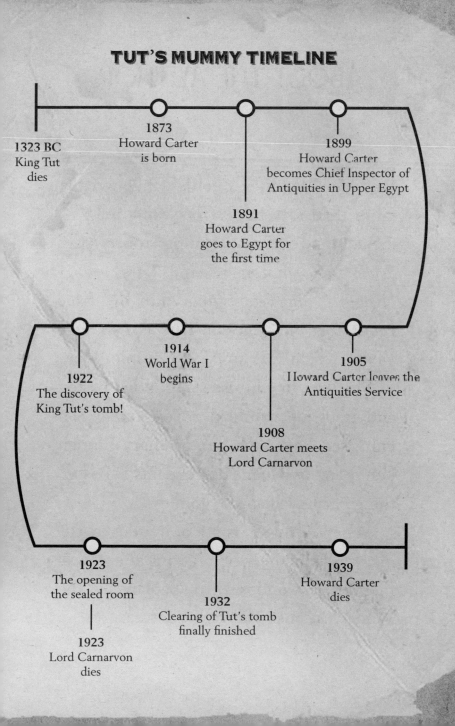

TUT'S MUMMY TIMELINE

1323 BC
King Tut
dies

1873
Howard Carter
is born

1891
Howard Carter
goes to Egypt for
the first time

1899
Howard Carter
becomes Chief Inspector of
Antiquities in Upper Egypt

1905
Howard Carter leaves the
Antiquities Service

1908
Howard Carter meets
Lord Carnarvon

1914
World War I
begins

1922
The discovery of
King Tut's tomb!

1923
The opening of
the sealed room

1923
Lord Carnarvon
dies

1932
Clearing of Tut's tomb
finally finished

1939
Howard Carter
dies

ABOUT THE AUTHOR

Kathleen Weidner Zoehfeld has written more than fifty books for young readers, including two other Stepping Stones, *Fossil Fever* and *Amazon Fever; Wild Lives: A History of the People and Animals of the Bronx Zoo;* and *Dinosaur Parents, Dinosaur Young,* which was an ALA Notable Book.

She lives in a house surrounded by fog and trees, on a hillside overlooking San Francisco Bay, with her ordinary human family and two feline descendants of Bastet, the great Egyptian cat goddess.

When Kathleen is not at her desk writing, you'll find her volunteering at her local museum or wandering the badlands of the Wild West in search of fossil treasures.